A Stu

IN SEARCH OF HOLINESS

David K. Bernard

A Study Guide for
In Search of Holiness
by David K. Bernard and Melanie Johnston
©Copyright 2011 David K. Bernard

Cover Design by Tim Cummings

Printed in United States of America.

WORD AFLAME PRESS
8855 Dunn Road, Hazelwood, MO 63042
www.pentecostalpublishing.com

Library of Congress Cataloging-in-Publication Data

Bernard, David K., 1956-
  A study guide for In search of holiness / David K. Bernard, Loretta A. Bernard. -- Rev. ed.
      p. cm. -- (Pentecostal theology ; v. 3)
  Rev. ed. of: In search of holiness / by Loretta A. Bernard and David K. Bernard.
  Includes index.
  ISBN 978-1-56722-949-3
  1. Christian life--Pentecostal authors. 2. Holiness--Pentecostal churches. I. Bernard, Loretta A. II. Bernard, Loretta A. In search of holiness. III. Title.
  BV4501.3.B473 2011
  248.4'8994--dc23
                        2011038031

Contents

Preface

This is a companion study guide to *In Search of Holiness* by David K. Bernard and Loretta A. Bernard. It is designed to be used for independent study, group Bible studies, Sunday school, church day schools, evening institutes, Bible colleges, seminars, and other training programs. The level of instruction can be adapted to the type of use.

This study guide outlines each section of *In Search of Holiness*. The outline is designed for a teacher to use in lecturing or for a student to use in personal study. It does not cover every detail of the book, but seeks to cover the most important points.

Each section of the outline concludes with study questions over important concepts. These questions call for short answers or discussion, and they can be used for independent study, homework, discussion, quizzes, or tests. Answers to the questions can be found in the back of the study guide, along with citations to relevant page numbers in *In Search of Holiness*. The outlines and questions and answers were prepared by Melanie Johnston. It is hoped this study guide will be a useful tool for both teacher and student as they study the doctrine of holiness.

OUTLINE
WITH
STUDY
QUESTIONS

1
HOLINESS: AN INTRODUCTION

A. Holiness defined

B. We must pursue holiness in order to see the Lord (Hebrews 12:14; John 3:3).

C. The need for separation

D. Holiness
1. Is imparted by the Holy Spirit
2. Is taught by the Bible
3. Is taught by Spirit-filled pastors and teachers
4. Is taught directly by the Spirit within us
5. Is an individual matter

E. Personal convictions
1. Cannot be legislated
2. Are maintained by love for God

F. Principles of holiness
1. We must not imitate the world of sin
2. We should exercise self-control and restraint

G. Attitudes
1. The Christian's attitude toward sin
2. The preacher's attitude toward sin

H. Preachers are messengers, not the author

I. Verses for victorious Christians to understand
    1. "The law of sin" (Romans 7:23)
    2. "The law of the Spirit" (Romans 8:2)
    3. "Whosoever is born of God doth not commit sin" (I John 3:9)
    4. "Dead to sin" (Romans 6:2)
    5. Separation from God (Romans 8:38-39)
    6. "If we say that we have no sin, we deceive ourselves" (I John 1:8)

J. Do Christians remain sinners?

K. Personal prayer

L. Filthiness of the flesh and spirit

M. Satan's message

N. Perfection
    1. Tolerance because of different levels of perfection
    2. "Let us go on unto perfection" (Hebrews 6:1)

Questions

1. Define holiness in reference to God.

2. Define holiness in reference to persons or objects.

3. What did holiness include for Old Testament Hebrews?

4. What does holiness include for born-again Christians?

5. If we are to have communion with God, what must we do?

6. What is sanctification, and how does it begin?

7. How does the Bible teach us holiness?

8. Why has God given the church pastors and teachers?

9. How does the indwelling of the Spirit help us obtain holiness?

10. How is holiness formed in the heart?

11. What are two basic principles of holiness?
    a.

    b.

12. When preachers are filled to overflowing with the Holy Spirit, how will they preach?

13. List six verses that are important for victorious Christians to understand.
    a.

    b.

    c.

    d.

    e.

    f.

14. Although Christians will still struggle with our sinful nature, what are we not to do?

15. If we fall under the influence of our sinful nature, what are we to do?

16. Explain the difference between absolute perfection and relative perfection.

2
THE CHRISTIAN LIFE

A. Basic concepts of Christian living

B. The purpose for holiness in our lives

C. Faith and works

D. The work of the Spirit

E. Christian characteristics
    1. Love
    2. Joy
    3. Peace
    4. Longsuffering and patience
    5. Gentleness
    6. Goodness
    7. Faith
    8. Meekness
    9. Temperance

F. Wisdom in dealing with people

G. Holiness as a way of life

Questions

1. List three reasons for holiness in our lives.
   a.

   b.

   c.

2. What is the proper motivation for holiness?

3. Explain the purpose of each of the following characteristics.
   a. Love:

   b. Joy:

   c. Peace:

   d. Longsuffering and patience:

   e. Gentleness:

   f. Goodness:

   g. Faith:

   h. Meekness:

   i. Temperance:

4. What is important when working with new converts?

5. How can holiness become a normal way of life?

3
CHRISTIAN ATTITUDES

A. Attitudes are the most important element of holiness

B. Love

C. Dangerous attitudes
1. Bitterness
2. Wrath
3. Anger
4. Clamor
5. Evil speaking
6. Malice
7. Envy and jealousy

D. Forgiveness

E. A root of bitterness

F. Nothing shall offend

G. Attitude when corrected

H. Murmuring and complaining

I. Busybodies

J. Pride

K. The feminist movement

L. Church meetings

M. The most important aspect of holiness

Questions

1. What is the basic attitude that distinguishes true Christians from the world?

2. What are the two commandments that can sum up the law and the prophets?
   a.

   b.

3. Name two ways to apply the teachings of love to the subject of holiness.
   a.

   b.

4. Define the following dangerous attitudes.
   a. Bitterness:

   b. Wrath:

   c. Anger:

   d. Clamor:

   e. Evil speaking:

   f. Malice:

   g. Envy and jealousy:

5. What does Scripture exhort us to do in place of all evil attitudes?

6. What is the most important part of forgiveness?

7. What is important to remember when we are hurt because we have been rebuked, misunderstood, or overlooked?

8. Name the five principles that Hebrews 13:17 teaches.
   a.

   b.

   c.

   d.

   e.

9. If there is a problem between two people, what should they do?

10. What is one of the three basic categories of worldliness that tempt Christians?

11. How can we eradicate pride?

12. In regard to church meetings, how should majority decisions be accepted?

13. What is the most important aspect of holiness?

4
THE TONGUE: UNRULY MEMBER

A. Unruly member

B. Ways people sin with the tongue
    1. Talebearing or gossip
    2. Sowing discord
    3. Swearing
    4. Taking God's name in vain
    5. Slang
    6. Filthy communication
    7. Cursing
    8. Reviling
    9. Lying and bearing false witness
    10. Careless words

C. Importance of the tongue

Questions

1. What is a good indication of an individual's relationship with God?

2. What does it signify when we speak in tongues for the first time under the inspiration of the Spirit?

3. What is Satan's primary tool for destroying the church from within?

4. What steps should we take if we hear someone has said or done something against us?
   a.

   b.

   c.

5. What is an abomination?

6. What does it mean to sow discord?

7. Why are we commanded not to swear?

8. What does the commandment "Thou shalt not take the name of the Lord thy God in vain" prohibit?

9. List four verses that speak about cursing people.

   a.

   b.
   c.

   d.

10. What does it mean to revile?

11. What is the proper reaction when others revile us?

12. List two verses that show God hates lies.

   a.

   b.

13. Why should we avoid speaking carelessly?

5
THE EYE: LIGHT OF THE BODY

A. Gate of the soul

B. Important passages of Scripture

C. Reading

D. Viewing

E. The problem with television, movies, and other media

    1. Michael and Diane Medved, *Saving Childhood*

    2. Marie Winn, *The Plug-In Drug*

    3. TV Turnoff Network

    4. American Academy of Pediatrics, *Television and the Family*

    5. Other research

K. Summary and response to objections

L. Conclusion

Questions

1. Define vanity.

2. As estimated by psychologists, what percentage of our thought life is stimulated by what we see?

3. Why does Satan try to bring temptations before our eyes?
   a.

   b.

   c.

   d.

4. What should we ask when in doubt about whether to read something or not?

5. What percent of Hollywood movies are rated G (general audiences)?

6. What fraction of Hollywood movies are rated R (restricted)?

7. What are the problems with television, movies, and other media?
   a.

   b.

8. How many hours per day is TV on in the average home?

9. How many hours per week does the average person watch TV?

10. What amount of their waking hours are preschool children in America spending watching TV?

11. How many more hours do children spend watching TV in the course of their school careers than they spend in the classroom?

12. List some adverse spiritual, mental, emotional, and physical effects of television.

6
SCRIPTURAL APPAREL
AND ADORNMENT

A. Outward appearance
   1. Modesty
   2. Avoiding personal ornamentation
   3. Moderation in cost
   4. Distinction between male and female
      a. Deuteronomy 22:5 applies today
      b. New Testament teaching on distinction between male and female
      c. Modern application of distinction in dress
   5. Separation from the world

B. Colored makeup and tattoos

C. Ornamental jewelry

D. Guidelines for children

E. A witness in early church history

F. A contemporary non-Pentecostal witness

G. The challenge today

Questions

1. List two reasons why it is important to understand principles of outward appearance.
   a.

   b.

2. What is the Greek word for "modest" and what does it mean?

3. What does "modest apparel" mean?

4. Define shamefacedness.

5. Define sobriety.

6. What is a good test to determine whether or not we are following the principle of moderation in cost?

7. What are the two social methods that God has established for maintaining the distinction between male and female?
   a.

   b.

8. What does I Corinthians 11 teach about men and woman's hair length?

9. What is the distinctive clothing of men in Western culture?

10. What is the distinctive clothing of women in Western culture?

11. When did the practice of women wearing pants gain acceptance in America?

12. In the Old Testament and throughout history, with what is painting the face associated?

13. According to I Timothy 2:9-10, how are women to adorn themselves?

14. According to I Timothy 2:9-10, how are women not to adorn themselves?

7
BIBLE TRUTHS CONCERNING HAIR

A. Reasons why a woman should have long hair

B. Reasons why a man should have short hair

C. Significance of hair in the Old Testament
   1. Hair was a symbol of perfection and strength
   2. Cutting of hair was a symbol of disgrace or mourning
   3. Hair was a symbol of glory
   4. Uncut hair was a mark of separation unto God

D. New Testament teaching

E. Reasons for biblical teaching on hair

F. How long is long?

G. Dyeing the hair

H. Attitudes

I. Shall we obey I Corinthians 11:1-16?

Questions

1. List six reasons why a woman should have long hair.
   a.

   b.

   c.

   d.

   e.

   f.

2. List five reasons why a man should have short hair.
   a.

   b.

   c.

   d.

   e.

3. What did an abundance of hair indicate among the Jews?

4. What were the three outward signs that separated Nazarites unto Jehovah?
   a.

   b.

   c.

5. How does nature teach women to grow their hair long and men to cut their hair short?
   a.

   b.

   c.

6. What is defined as "long hair?"

7. What are the two concerns regarding a woman's attitude toward long hair?
   a.

   b.

8
THE TEMPLE OF GOD

A. The body

B. Food
  1. Blood
  2. Food offered to idols
  3. Temperance and gluttony

C. Beverages

D. Alcoholic beverages

E. Drugs and narcotics

F. Tobacco

G. Conclusion

Questions

1. How did the law of Moses restrict the diet of Israel?

2. What were the purposes of these dietary laws?
   a.

   b.

3. What four points of the Jewish law did the leaders of the New Testament church decide that Gentile Christians needed to keep?
   a.

   b.

   c.

   d.

4. Why are we not to eat blood?

5. Why should we practice good eating habits?

6. What are the evil consequences of drinking wine and mixed wine?

7. What are the two Hebrew words for "wine" and what do they each mean?
   a.

   b.

8. What are the two Greek words for "wine" and what do they each mean?

    a.

    b.

9. What are the biblical and social arguments for abstention from alcoholic beverages?

    a.

    b.

    c.

10. What does the use of marijuana cause?

11. What is the leading cause of lung cancer and emphysema?

12. What percentage of all adult deaths are caused by tobacco?

9
SEXUAL RELATIONSHIPS

A. Marriage

B. Sexual sins
   1. Fornication
   2. Adultery
   3. Incest
   4. Child molestation
   5. Bestiality
   6. Rape
   7. Lust
   8. Lewdness and uncleanness
   9. Pornography

C. Overcoming lust

D. Masturbation (self-stimulation)

E. Effeminate behavior

F. Homosexual behavior
   1. Factors that influence homosexual behavior
   2. Overcoming homosexual behavior

G. Conclusion

Questions

1. What was God's purpose in ordaining marriage?

2. What is the purpose of a sexual relationship?

3. Why are sexual sins particularly serious?

4. Define fornication.

5. How many laws are there in the Bible defining the sin of incest?

6. How does temptation become sin?

7. How can the sin of pornography be avoided?

8. What are the two potential problems that result from masturbation?
   a.

   b.

9. Why is homosexuality contrary to nature?

10. What does Romans 1 reveal about homosexuality?

11. What are some factors that can increase a person's susceptibility to homosexual temptations?

12. Why is homosexuality such a powerful force?
    a.

    b.

    c.

13. What are the steps to overcoming homosexuality?
    a.

    b.

    c.

10
ABSTAINING
FROM BLOODSHED

A. A basic law

B. Murder

C. Hatred

D. Warfare and self-defense

E. Abortion

F. Suicide

G. Conclusion

Questions

1. Why is it wrong to kill another human being?
   a.

   b.

   c.

2. What must we do instead of letting hatred lodge in our hearts?

3. How can we support our nation in times of war?

4. According to the Bible, does God consider a child in the womb to be human?

5. What should we do if problems overwhelm us and suicide becomes a temptation?

11
HONESTY
AND INTEGRITY

A. Theft

B. Fraud

C. Work ethic

D. Paying taxes

E. Paying debts

F. Making and guaranteeing loans

G. Extortion

H. Usury and interest

1. Bribes and gifts

J. Honesty and integrity today

Questions

1. What is the proper way to obtain what we need?

2. What are we doing when we refuse to pay tithes?

3. What does it mean to defraud?

4. How should Christians endeavor to act in the workplace?

5. What should full-time ministers ask themselves for self-evaluation of their work ethic?

6. What are we doing if we refuse to pay the taxes we owe?

7. What must we do if we borrow?

8. What does it mean to extort?

9. When is giving a gift wrong?

12
AUTHORITY
AND ORGANIZATION
IN THE CHURCH

A. Authority in the church
    1. Organization in the early church
    2. The authority of leadership

B. Judgment in the church

C. Lawsuits

D. Church discipline

E. Public rebuke

F. "Touch not mine anointed"

G. Errors in leadership

H. Independence

I. Benefits of unity

Questions

1. Upon what is the church founded?

2. In Acts chapter 2, what did the people do after the outpouring of the Holy Spirit?

3. Why is laying on of hands administered?

4. What took place in Acts 15?

5. Why do we esteem people in authority?

6. What is the purpose of leadership in the church?

7. What is the procedure that Jesus gave in case of a conflict between two believers?
   a.

   b.

   c.

   d.

8. What happens when people who are recognized as church members live in open, notorious, unrepented sin?

9. What is the best way to handle problems when they arise?

10. What is an example of a situation that must be addressed publicly for the good of the body?

11. What does I Chronicles 16:22 tell us that God will do?

12. What should we do if a leader is operating unethically, living in sin, or teaching false doctrine?

13. What does good organization do?

14. How does a large fellowship help keep local groups in the mainstream of God's will?

13
FELLOWSHIP
AND ALLIANCES

A. Fellowship with the world

B. Fellowship with sinners in the church

C. Unequally yoked with unbelievers

D. Definition of a believer

E. Old Testament examples

F. Marriage

G. Dating

Questions

1. How will we be affected if we associate closely with evil people?

2. If we expect to win souls, what must we do?

3. What are the two areas of fellowship in which the Bible gives specific directions?
   a.

   b.

4. List the types of sinners with whom we should not associate closely if they profess to be believers:
   a.

   b.

   c.

   d.

   e.

   f.

   g.

   h.

5. What do false teachers typically manifest or cause?

6. To what does the yoke relationship refer?

7. What is the most obvious example of a yoke relationship?

8. What is the biblical proof of belief?

9. To what does becoming yoked with unbelievers lead?

10. What kind of partners should Christians choose?

14
WORSHIP,
EMOTIONS, AND MUSIC

A. True worship

B. Emotions and expression

C. Examples of worship

D. Quenching the Spirit

E. Music in worship

F. Modern music

Questions

1. What is the truest form of worship?

2. To what does emotion lead?

3. According to Psalms, what are some examples of appropriate praise in the congregation?

4. How is the Spirit sometimes quenched?

5. What can the right kind of music accomplish?

6. List the instruments used in Psalm 150 for worship:
   a.

   b.

   c.

   d.

   e.

   f.

   g.

   h.

7. In church, what should be the primary goal of singers and musicians?

8. In church, what should be the secondary goal of singers and musicians?

9. When is true worship hindered?

15
WORLDLY PLEASURES

A. Guidelines
   1. Amusement
   2. Atmosphere
   3. Appearance

B. Gambling

C. Dancing

D. Sports

E. Witchcraft
   1. Superstition
   2. Satan's power

F. Summary

Questions

1. What does the Bible warn us that people will do in the last days when they get caught up in pleasure?

2. According to II Timothy 3:2 and 3:4, what is a key sign of the end times?

3. How can the world corrupt wholesome and enjoyable activities?

4. When we do our best to follow godly principles and make godly choices in areas under our control, what can we trust God to do?

5. In situations that could appear worldly, what should we do?

6. Of what is gambling a combination?

7. To what is gambling an appeal?

8. What is the primary motivation behind most forms of social dancing in modern Western culture?

9. When sports become highly organized in a secular environment, what problems can result?

a.

b.

c.

d.

e.

f.

10. To what does witchcraft refer?

11. According to Deuteronomy 18:9-12 the activities of the following people are abominations to God?

a.

b.

c.

d.

e.

f.

g.

h.

I.

12. What was the test of false prophets?

16
PRACTICAL SUGGESTIONS

A. General suggestions

B. Twenty practical guidelines

Questions

1. List the twenty practical guidelines for helping us to perfect holiness:

   a.

   b.

   c.

   d.

   e.

   f.

   g.

   h.

   i.

   j.

   k.

   i.

   m.

   n.

   o.

   p.

   q.

r.

s.

t.

ANSWERS
TO
STUDY
QUESTIONS

(Page numbers refer to
In Search of Holiness)

1

1. Holiness in reference to God means absolute perfection and purity. (p. 11)
2. Holiness in reference to persons or objects means what has been separated or set apart unto God. (p. 11)
3. Holiness for the Old Testament Hebrews included the negative concept of "separation" and the positive concept of "dedication." (p. 11)
4. For born-again Christians, holiness includes separation from sin and the world and dedication to God and His will. (p. 11)
5. If we are to have communion with God, we must separate ourselves from the old life of sin. (p. 12)
6. Sanctification is separation from sin and it begins with the hearing of the gospel and continues through faith, repentance, and water baptism in Jesus' name. It is accomplished primarily by the indwelling of the Holy Spirit. (p. 13)
7. The Bible teaches us holiness by giving us basic guidelines that apply to men and women of all cultures, times, and situations, and teaches practices and attitudes that God accepts and those He expects. (p. 13)
8. God has given the church pastors and teachers for the perfecting, or equipping, of the saints so that the church can grow to maturity. (p. 13)
9. The indwelling of the Spirit helps us obtain holiness by assisting us to make correct decisions in particular situations. (p. 14)
10. Holiness is formed in the heart through the teaching of the Word of God and the work of the Holy Spirit. (p. 15)

11. Two basic principles of holiness:
    a. We must not imitate the world of sin.
    b. We should exercise self-control and restraint. (p. 16)
12. When preachers are filled to overflowing with the Holy Spirit, they will preach boldly against sin but will also manifest the genuine love of God for sinners. (p. 18)
13. Six verses that are important for victorious Christians to understand:
    a. Romans 7:23
    b. Romans 8:2 (p. 19)
    c. I John 3:9
    d. Romans 6:2 (p. 20)
    e. Romans 8:38-39
    f. I John 1:8 (p. 21)
14. Although Christians will still struggle with our sinful nature, we are not to sin habitually or live in a sinful state. (p. 22)
15. If we fall under the influence of our sinful nature, we are to confess our sins to Jesus Christ immediately. (p. 22)
16. Jesus Christ alone exemplifies absolute perfection. Relative perfection is what is achieved when we are growing properly during the process of perfection. (p. 24)

2

1. Three reasons for holiness in our lives:
   a. To please God.
   b. To communicate Christ to others.
   c. For our own benefit. (p. 28)
2. The proper motivation for holiness is faith in God. (p. 28)
3. The purpose of the following characteristics are:

a. Love: Love is the most basic element of our Christian life. It is the only acceptable motivation for serving God. (p. 31)
b. Joy: Joy is a weapon and a source of strength. (p. 32)
c. Peace: No matter what happens, we can have inner peace. We can also have peace with others. (p. 32)
d. Longsuffering and patience: With patience we bear fruit, run our race, and obtain promises by faith. (p. 33)
e. Gentleness: Gentleness will make us great. To be gentle is to be courteous, mannerly, kind, patient, and serene. (p. 34)
f. Goodness: We are saved as we continue in God's goodness. (p. 34)
g. Faith: We need faith to be saved and to continue in our Christian walk. (p. 34)
h. Meekness: With meekness we are to preach the Word, receive the Word, help and restore an erring brother, display wisdom, and adorn our lives. (p. 35)
i. Temperance: We need to display temperance at all times. It encompasses self-restraint, self-control, and moderation. (p. 36)
4. When working with new converts, patience and tolerance are important. They need positive teaching, encouragement, and understanding. (p. 37)
5. Holiness can become a normal way of life if we let God's Spirit lead us and if we will cultivate the fruit of the Spirit, then the pursuit of holiness will not be difficult. It will be a joy and not a burden. (p. 39)

3

1. The basic attitude that distinguishes true Christians from the world is love. (p. 41)
2. The two commandments that can sum up the law and the prophets:
   a. Love God.
   b. Love our fellow humans. (p. 42)
3. Two ways to apply the teachings of love to the subject of holiness:
   a. We should love God enough to do His perfect will. (p. 42)
   b. We should be on guard when any type of resentment or dislike arises in us toward another human being. (p. 43)
4. The definitions of the following characteristics are:
   a. Bitterness: Something sharp, disagreeable, distasteful, harsh, severe, resentful, or vehement. (p. 43)
   b. Wrath: Violent anger, rage, or indignation. (p. 44)
   c. Anger: A feeling of extreme displeasure that usually results from injury or opposition. (p. 44)
   d. Clamor: Noisy shouting, outcry, uproar, or insistent demand. (p. 45)
   e. Evil speaking: Comes from an evil heart. (p. 45)
   f. Malice: Active ill will, a desire to hurt others. (p. 45)
   g. Envy and jealousy: Envy is resentment or ill will because of the advantages, possessions, or accomplishments of someone else. Jealousy is a resentful suspicion or envy. (p. 46)

5. In place of all evil attitudes, Scripture exhorts us to be kind to one another, tenderhearted and forgiving. (p. 46)
6. The most important part of forgiveness is a decision to forget. (p. 46)
7. When we are hurt because we have been rebuked, misunderstood, or overlooked, it's important to remember that nothing shall offend. (p. 49)
8. The five principles that Hebrews 13:17 teaches:
   a. God has ordained leaders in the church.
   b. We are to be humble and obedient.
   c. True leaders have a duty to watch over our souls. (p. 50)
   d. Leaders are responsible to God.
   e. God will be our judge. (p. 51)
9. If there is a problem between two people, they should seek reconciliation without spreading the problem to others. (p. 52)
10. One of the three basic categories of worldliness that tempt Christians is the pride of life. (p. 55)
11. We can eradicate pride through prayer. (p. 56)
12. In regard to church meetings, majority decisions should be accepted with a good attitude, without murmuring, complaining, or sowing discord. (p. 59)
13. The most important aspect of holiness is a proper attitude. (p. 60)

4

1. A good indication of an individual's relationship with God is the way he uses the tongue. (p. 61)

2. When we speak in tongues for the first time under the inspiration of the Spirit, it signifies that God has at last come inside and taken complete control. (p. 62)

3. Satan's primary tool for destroying the church from within is talebearing or gossip. (p. 62)

4. The steps should we take if we hear that someone has said or done something against us:
   a. We should not be quick to believe the rumor. (p. 65)
   b. If the report still bothers us, we should pray for the Lord to give us peace.
   c. If the problem persists even after prayer, we should go to the person who is involved, get the story straight from him or her, and clear up the problem. (p. 66)

5. An abomination is something God hates. (p. 67)

6. To sow discord means to cause dislike, distrust, and division, and it often occurs by talebearing or constant criticism. (p. 67)

7. We are commanded to not swear because we cannot control the things we swear upon. (p. 68)

8. The commandment "Thou shalt not take the name of the Lord thy God in vain" prohibits all profane, meaningless, trivial, or irreverent use of God's name. (p. 69)

9. Four verses that speak about cursing people:
   a. Romans 12:14
   b. James 3:10
   c. Romans 12:21
   d. Matthew 5:44 (p. 71)

10. To revile means to abuse using words; to use harsh, insolent, or abusive language. (p. 73)

11. The proper reaction when others revile us is to bless them. (p. 73)
12. Two verses that show that God hates lies:
    a. Exodus 20:16
    b. Revelation 21:8 (p. 76)
13. We should avoid speaking carelessly because if we speak carelessly, we could easily commit sin and could easily harm others. (p. 79)

5

1. Vanity is anything that is worthless, foolish, empty, and destitute of reality. (p. 81)
2. Ninety percent of our thought life is stimulated by what we see. (p. 82)
3. Reasons Satan tries to bring temptations before our eyes:
    a. We encounter suggestions that we had not previously known about or considered.
    b. Scenes can become embedded in our memories so that they are available to tempt us later when we are weak or discouraged.
    c. Constant exposure to certain sights and their associated ideas causes us gradually to become accustomed to them.
    d. If we think about certain things long enough, we will eventually sin. (p. 83)
4. When in doubt about whether to read something or not, we should ask, "Are these meditations acceptable in the sight of God?" (p. 85)
5. Three percent of Hollywood movies are rated G (general audiences). (p. 87)
6. Two-thirds of Hollywood movies are rated R (restricted). (p. 87)

7. The problems with television, movies, and other media:
   a. The kinds of things displayed on the screen are generally not conducive to Christian living. (p. 89)
   b. Television is mostly a waste of time. (p. 90)
8. The television is on in the average home for 7.28 hours per day. (p. 92)
9. The average person watches television for 24 hours per week. (p. 92)
10. Preschool children in America are spending one quarter of their waking hours watching television. (p. 93)
11. Children spend 4,000 more hours watching television in the course of their school careers than they spend in the classroom. (p. 94)
12. Some adverse spiritual, mental, emotional, and physical effects of television are that it feeds the lusts of the flesh, is a constant source of temptation, is a thief of time, harms family life, warps children's character and morals, promotes sin, and is psychologically detrimental. (p. 99)

6

1. Two reasons why it is important to understand principles of outward appearance:
   a. Styles of dress and customs have changed since the days of the Bible (p. 103)
   b. Few statements in the New Testament specifically deal with men's appearance, since men's adornment was generally not a problem in those days. (p. 104)

2. The Greek word for "modest" is *kosmios*, and it means "orderly, well-arranged, decent, modest." (p. 104)

3. Modest apparel means clothing that does not indecently expose the body to the opposite sex, whether intentionally or carelessly. (p. 105)

4. Shamefacedness means reverence, self-restraint, modesty, and bashfulness. (pp. 105-106)

5. Sobriety means discretion, temperance, and self-control. (p. 106)

6. A good test to determine whether or not we are following the principle of moderation in cost is to ask if certain clothing would be an ostentatious display of wealth in the sight of acquaintances and fellow believers. (p. 106)

7. The two social methods that God has established for maintaining the distinction between male and female:
   a. Dress
   b. Hair length (p. 107)

8. I Corinthians 11 teaches that men should have short hair and women should have long hair. (p. 109)

9. The distinctive clothing of men in Western culture is pants. (p. 110)

10. The distinctive clothing of women in Western culture is dresses and skirts. (p. 110)

11. The practice of women wearing pants gained acceptance in America during World War II. (p. 111)

12. In the Old Testament and throughout history, painting the face has been associated with brazenness, forwardness, seduction, and prostitution. (p. 114)

13. According to I Timothy 2:9-10, women are to adorn themselves in modest clothing and with good works. (p. 116)
14. According to I Timothy 2:9-10, women are not to adorn themselves with broided hair, or gold, or pearls, or costly array. (p. 116)

7

1. Six reasons why a woman should have long hair:
   a. Long hair is a sign of her submission to authority.
   b. The angels are watching to see if she has this sign.
   c. It is a shame for a woman to pray or prophesy with an uncovered head, for she thereby dishonors her head (authority). Long hair is her symbolic head covering. If she shears (cuts) her hair it is like shaving her head. (p. 125)
   d. Nature teaches her to have long hair as opposed to shorn (cut) hair or a shaved head.
   e. Long hair is a woman's glory.
   f. It is one of God's methods for maintaining a distinction between male and female. (p. 126)
2. Five reasons why a man should have short hair:
   a. Short hair on a man is a symbol of his position of authority and his submission to Christ's authority.
   b. A man who prays or prophesies with his head covered by long hair dishonors his head (authority), which is Christ.
   c. Nature teaches him to have short hair.

   d. Long hair is a shame on a man.

   e. It is one of God's methods for maintaining a distinction between male and female. (p. 126)

3. An abundance of hair among the Jews indicated perfection and strength. (p. 126)

4. The three outward signs that separated Nazarites unto Jehovah:

   a. A Nazarite was not to partake of grapes or any product of grapes.

   b. A Nazarite was not to touch a corpse.

   c. A Nazarite was not to cut the hair on the head. (p. 128)

5. Hair symbolizes the relationship of husband and wife, which in turn represents the Lord's relationship with the church. (p. 133)

6. Ways nature teaches women to grow their hair long and men to cut their hair short:

   a. Nature teaches that there should be a visible distinction between male and female.

   b. In almost all cultures, men have worn short hair in comparison to women.

   c. Men are ten times more likely to go bald than women. (p. 133)

7. "Long hair" is defined as uncut hair or hair that is allowed to grow freely. (p. 134)

8. The two concerns regarding a woman's attitude toward long hair:

   a. Some may resent the need to care for and fix long hair.

   b. Pride. (p. 136)

8

1. The law of Moses restricted the diet of Israel by forbidding Israelites to eat camel, coney,

hare, pig, aquatic animals without scales and fins, twenty different kinds of birds (mostly scavengers and birds of prey), and all insects except locusts, bald locusts, and beetles. (p. 140)

2. The purposes of these dietary laws:
   a. To separate Israel from all other nations.
   b. To protect the Israelites from unsanitary and disease-carrying food. (p. 140)

3. The four points of the Jewish law that the leaders of the New Testament church decided that Gentile Christians needed to keep:
   a. Abstain from food offered to idols.
   b. Abstain from fornication.
   c. Abstain from things strangled.
   d. Abstain from blood. (p. 141)

4. We are not to eat blood because God has chosen blood to represent life and to represent remission of sins in every age. (p. 142)

5. We should practice good eating habits to preserve our health and strength. (p. 144)

6. The consequences of drinking wine and mixed wine are woe, sorrow, contention, babbling, wounds, bloodshot eyes, sexual sin, indecent talk, loss of balance and coordination, insensibility, and addiction. (p. 146)

7. The two Hebrew words for "wine" and what they each mean:
   a. *Yayin*: can refer to any type of wine, but usually means fermented wine. (p. 147)

b. *Tiyrosh*: almost always refers to newly made, unfermented wine. (p. 148)

8. The two Greek words for "wine" and what they each mean:

    a. *Oinos*: usually refers to fermented wine, but can also refer to unfermented wine.

    b. *Gleukos*: can mean freshly made wine or sweet wine. (p. 148)

9. The biblical and social arguments for abstention from alcoholic beverages:

    a. It is practically impossible for people to drink so little that they are never affected mentally or never get drunk. (p. 152)

    b. Not everyone can resist the temptation presented by a drink, and not everyone can handle even a small amount of alcohol.

    c. The Bible tells us to avoid all appearance of evil. (p. 152)

10. The use of marijuana causes lack of self-control, can cause psychological addiction, and can lead to use of hard drugs. (p. 153)

11. The leading cause of lung cancer and emphysema is smoking. (p. 154)

12. Ten percent of all adult deaths are caused by tobacco. (p. 154)

9

1. God's purpose in ordaining marriage was to provide for companionship, communion, and partnership between husband and wife and to devise a method of procreation. (pp. 157-158)

2. The purpose of a sexual relationship is for the consummation and strengthening of the union of a man and a woman, as well as for procreation. (p. 158)

3. Sexual sins are particularly serious because they violate the sacredness of marriage. (p. 159)

4. Fornication means all sexual intercourse outside a biblical marriage, including oral and anal sex. (p. 161)
5. There are twenty laws in the Bible defining the sin of incest. (p. 161)
6. Temptation becomes sin if we entertain it and allow it to develop into lust. (p. 162)
7. The sin of pornography can be avoided by placing controls on media and maintaining spiritual disciplines. (p. 163)
8. The two potential problems that result from masturbation:
   a. Lustful fantasies.
   b. Addictive behavior. (p. 165)
9. Homosexuality is contrary to nature because it involves use of the body contrary to God's design. (p. 169)
10. Romans 1 reveals that homosexuality is the final depravity that results when humans persistently refuse to worship God. (p. 170)
11. Some factors that can increase a person's susceptibility to homosexual temptations are characteristics of culture, personality, physique, background, or life experience. (p. 171)
12. Reasons homosexuality is such a powerful force:
    a. It typically results from early life experiences that are hard to erase.
    b. It has usually developed over a long period of time and has become an ingrained habit.
    c. Spiritual forces are involved. (p. 176)
13. The steps to overcoming homosexuality:
    a. Cease homosexual activities.
    b. Seek deliverance from homosexual desires.

c. For God to give the normal heterosexual desires He intends for all to have. (p. 177)

10

1. Reasons it is wrong to kill another human being:
   a. It is a sin against God. (p. 181)
   b. It is a sin against family and society.
   c. It is a sin against the victims. (p. 182)
2. Instead of letting hatred lodge in our hearts, we must resolve conflicts, get rid of grudges, and do what we can to live in peace with others. (p. 183)
3. We can support our nation in times of war through noncombatant roles and roles that help preserve life, such as medical personnel, supply personnel, and chaplains. (p. 183)
4. According to the Bible, God does consider a child in the womb to be human. (p. 186)
5. If problems overwhelm us and suicide becomes a temptation, we should turn to God for strength. (p. 188)

11

1. The proper way to obtain what we need is to work for it. (p. 191)
2. When we refuse to pay tithes, we are robbing God. (p. 193)
3. To defraud means to cheat, swindle, take by trickery, or take by deception. (p. 194)
4. In the workplace, Christians should endeavor to come to work on time, depart on time,

make up for personal time if necessary, and obtain permission to take time off. (p. 196)

5. For self-evaluation of their work ethic, full-time ministers should ask themselves, "Apart from personal devotion and time spent in church services, do I spend at least forty hours a week actively working for the kingdom of God?" (p. 197)

6. If we refuse to pay the taxes we owe, we are defrauding the government and our fellow citizens. (p. 197)

7. If we borrow, we must repay and repay on time. (p. 198)

8. To extort means to obtain money or favors by violence, threat, or misuse of authority. (p. 201)

9. Giving a gift is wrong when the intention is to gain an unfair advantage or an unlawful favor in return. (p. 203)

12

1. The church is founded upon the Word of God. (p. 208)

2. After the outpouring of the Spirit in Acts chapter 2, the people "continued steadfastly in the apostles' doctrine and fellowship." (p. 208)

3. Laying on of hands is administered so that God will bless, heal, or anoint someone for a special purpose. (p. 209)

4. What could be called the first general conference of the church took place in Acts 15. (p. 210)

5. We esteem people in authority because God has given them authority to do their jobs. (p. 214)

6. The purpose of leadership in the church is "for the perfecting of the saints, for the work of the ministry, for the edifying of the body of Christ." (p. 214)

7. The procedure that Jesus gave in case of a conflict between two believers:

   a. The aggrieved party should go to the other person privately in an attempt to resolve the matter.

   b. If the attempt at resolution does not work, then the aggrieved person should take two or three witnesses with him in a second attempt to resolve the problem.

   c. If the problem is not resolved, then it should be brought to the church.

   d. If someone refuses to heed the judgment of the church, then he or she is to be removed from fellowship and considered to be an unbeliever. (p. 216)

8. When people who are recognized as church members live in open, notorious, unrepented sin, they present a false message to the world about what the church stands for. (p. 218)

9. The best way to handle problems when they arise is on an individual basis, as privately and discreetly as possible. (p. 222)

10. An example of a situation that must be addressed publicly for the good of the body is if someone must be removed from fellowship for notorious sin. (p. 222)

11. I Chronicles 16:22 tells us that God will protect His people and will punish those who attack them. God will support and defend His leaders. (p. 224)

12. If a leader is operating unethically, living in sin, or teaching false doctrine, we should not follow the leader in this area. We should bring the matter to the attention of those who have authority to deal with it. (p. 227)
13. Good organization promotes evangelism and outreach. (p. 229)
14. A large fellowship helps keep local groups in the mainstream of God's will because the diversity of viewpoints keeps the whole group in balance. (p. 230)

13

1. If we associate closely with evil people, we will be adversely affected. (p. 232)
2. We must associate with souls if we expect to win souls. (p. 232)
3. The two areas of fellowship in which the Bible gives specific directions:
   a. We must not have fellowship with people who call themselves Christians but who live in notorious sins.
   b. We must not become unequally yoked together with unbelievers. (p. 233)
4. The types of sinners with whom we should not associate closely if they profess to be believers:
   a. Fornicators.
   b. Covetous.
   c. Idolaters.
   d. Railers.
   e. Drunkards. (p. 236)
   f. Extortioners.
   g. Those who walk disorderly.
   h. False teachers. (p. 237)

5. False teachers typically manifest or cause envy, strife, railing, evil surmisings, and perverse disputings. (p. 238)
6. The yoke relationship refers to a close, intimate union in which one person can drastically affect or influence another, in which one person can speak or act for another, and in which there is a sharing of responsibility. (p. 241)
7. The most obvious example of a yoke relationship is marriage. (p. 241)
8. The biblical proof of belief is obedience to the Word of God. (p. 241)
9. Becoming yoked with unbelievers leads to compromise with the world. (p. 243)
10. Christians should choose partners who share the same basic experience, belief, and lifestyle. (p. 243)

14

1. The truest form of worship is obedience. (p. 247)
2. Emotion leads to physical expression. (p. 249)
3. According to Psalms, some examples of appropriate praise in the congregation are lifting of hands, singing and playing musical instruments, making a joyful noise, clapping hands, and dancing. (p. 249)
4. The Spirit is sometimes quenched formality and unscriptural traditions. (p. 251)
5. The right kind of music can help drive away worries and evil thoughts and can bring peace, encouragement, and closeness to God. (p. 252)

6. The instruments used in Psalm 150 for worship:
   a. Trumpet
   b. Psaltry
   c. Harp
   d. Timbrel
   e. Stringed instrument
   f. Organ
   g. Loud cymbal
   h. High-sounding cymbal (p. 252)
7. In church, the primary goal of singers and musicians should be to worship God from the heart, creating music that He is pleased to hear. (p. 255)
8. In church, the secondary goal of singers and musicians should be to create an atmosphere of worship that will encourage the congregation to worship and usher them into the presence of God. (p. 255)
9. True worship is hindered when the singers and musicians do not truly worship, when they perform for self-exaltation, or when they do not endeavor to live a holy life. (pp. 255-256)

15

1 The Bible warns us that in the last days people will be so caught up in pleasure that they will ignore and neglect God. (p. 261)
2. According to II Timothy 3:2 and 3:4, a key sign of the end times is "men shall be lovers of their own selves" and "lovers of pleasures more than lovers of God." (p. 261)

3. The world can corrupt wholesome and enjoyable activities by a worldly atmosphere. (p. 262)
4. When we do our best to follow godly principles and make godly choices in areas under our control, we can trust God to protect and preserve us from the evil influence of the world around us. (p. 263)
5. In situations that could appear worldly, we should take care not to damage our testimony or to cause a stumbling block for others. (p. 263)
6. Gambling is a combination of worldly amusement, atmosphere, and appearance. (p. 264)
7. Gambling is an appeal to greed. (p. 264)
8. The primary motivation behind most forms of social dancing in modern Western culture is sexuality. (p. 265)
9. When sports become highly organized in a secular environment, these problems can result:
   a. Competitive sports often demand excessive time and dedication.
   b. Participants may have to wear immodest or unisex clothing that is contrary to biblical teaching.
   c. Sometimes sports are conducted in a worldly atmosphere that is detrimental to both spectator and player.
   d. Too often, the result is to glorify violence. (p. 266)
   e. Modern organized sports tend to glorify the athletes.
   f. For many people, sports become an obsession, an addiction, or an idol. (p. 267)

10. Witchcraft refers to attempts to forecast, influence, or control events or forces by supernatural means. (p. 268)
11. The nine activities of the following people are abominations to God:
    a. Anyone who practices human sacrifice.
    b. Anyone who practices "divination."
    c. "Observer of times."
    d. "Enchanter."
    e. "Witch."
    f. "Charmer."
    g. "Consulter with familiar spirits."
    h. "Wizard."
    i. "Necromancer." (p. 269)
12. The test of false prophets was whether they worshiped the one true God. (p. 272)

16

1. The twenty practical guidelines for helping us to perfect holiness are:
    a. "Abstain from all appearance of evil."
    b. When in doubt about something, don't do it.
    c. Be kind and compassionate. (p. 278)
    d. Provide for your family.
    e. Be an example to the believer first.
    f. Love the teaching of God's Word. (p. 278)
    g. Don't listen to talebearing.
    h. Seek reconciliation.
    i. Don't become a stumbling block to other believers. (p. 280)
    j. Desire spiritual things.
    k. Beware of carnal human reasoning.
    l. Don't make excuses. (p. 281)
    m. Don't rely excessively on people, but look to the Lord for strength. (p. 282)

n. Control your spirit and your temper.
o. Guard your integrity and reputation.
p. Be humble. (p. 283)
q. Guard against the things God hates.
r. Have your own convictions, and be true to them. (p. 284)
s. Love God and hate evil.
t. Strive to be like Christ. (p. 285)